To Hélène...
For having allowed TOOLS OF THE HEART to exist
by your caring presence and unconditional support.
For your wisdom and advice at each step of the process.

To Michèle...
For conjugating simplicity and meaning in the words that
shaped this wonderful literary universe for children.

And...
For the dedication, the trust, the open-mindedness, the
perseverance and the synergy that prevailed during this
precious collaboration.

I offer all my joy and gratitude.
THANK YOU!!

Tools of the Heart

Fostering confidence and self-esteem

Father Sun and Mother Earth Create Life

Breathing/Finding your rhythm

Breathing is essential to life; conscious breathing is a simple, yet effective way to regain your calm and well-being by finding your body's rhythm.

Once upon a time, living among the stars, there was a beautiful blue planet called Earth. Nearby was a very big and bright star called the Sun.

The Sun was warm and comforting. The Earth was carrying a lot of water, which was covering most of her surface.

Every day they would spend a lot of time together.

As time passed by, they loved each other more and more every day. So they decided to grow a garden together.

They would come up with plenty of ideas for their garden and even found a name for it. They would call it *Life*!

The Earth then decided to share an important secret with the Sun;
«I discovered that there is a rainbow of wisdom in everyone's heart,» she said.

The Sun was deeply moved and overjoyed. Together, they kept planning and dreaming about their garden. The Earth would carry Life, while the Sun would cuddle her with love and support.

The Sun began to warm the Earth with greater energy, making the waters slowly evaporate. Sometimes, clouds would gather in the sky, and it would rain for days, but the soft warmth of the Sun would always return. The blue planet was changing, revealing more and more land.

At last, one day, the garden began to grow.

The Earth and the Sun were excited. They were finally a mom and a dad! They were beaming with love.

However, one morning, their garden did not look so well.
Worried, they asked a dear friend for help.

The Moon reassured her friends.

«By learning to breathe deeply, Mother Earth will allow the garden to bloom and flourish,» she said. «But how?» asked Mother Earth and Father Sun.

The Moon smiled and asked,
«Dear Earth, did you forget about
your rainbow of wisdom?»

Mother Earth closed her eyes to feel what was deep within her heart. She felt a soothing sensation, and her wisdom popped up, looking like a red elf.

Red guided the Earth how to breathe gently and deeply. He explained to her that when breathing in, she would feel her belly go out. Then, by breathing out, she would feel her belly go in.

By breathing this way and finding her rhythm, Mother Earth felt calmed and relaxed.

She felt so good after that; she wanted to share this discovery with everyone!

She talked to the garden about the rainbow of wisdom. She then explained how to go in one's heart to meet the red elf, who knows how to breathe in and out slowly and deeply.

Together, they learned how to breathe this way.

Inhale. Hmffffff...
Exhale. Pfffffffffff...

Inhale. Hmffffff...
Exhale. Pfffffffffff...

Inhale. Hmffffff...
Exhale. Pfffffffffff...

Everyone in the garden now knows about their rainbow of wisdom. When they feel the need to, they stop for a moment.

They close their eyes and breathe slowly and deeply to feel better, just like the red elf taught them.

High in the sky, stars celebrate with Father Sun and Mother Earth who embrace their garden with love.

Together, they continue to teach everyone in the garden how to breathe slowly and deeply.

As for the moon...
She is still there, happily gazing upon the sleeping garden.
She takes comfort in knowing that a heart full of love is an
extraordinary gift for life!

Remember...

How do I breathe in and out like Mother Earth?

Close your eyes and put one hand on your heart. Put the other hand on your belly. Inhale through your nose and exhale slowly. Feel your belly going in and out.
Repeat three times.

Why is it important to breathe deeply like that?

If you need a moment, breathing slowly and deeply will help your body to relax and feel energized again. This little moment of calmness can help you to find your rhythm and enjoy the rest of the day!

What if I'm too excited or fidgety?

When you take the time to breathe slowly and deeply, it helps you find your calm and your well-being, even if you feel too excited or fidgety.

Tools of the Heart

Fostering confidence and self-esteem

Fluffy and the Rainbow in his Heart

Meditation/Finding your inner calm

Each one of us has a peaceful place inside their heart. Meditation is a tool that allows you to find your personal space or to go back to it.

Father Sun and Mother Earth have created
a beautiful garden that they deeply love.
Their hearts are filled with joy.

However, from time to time, areas of shade were seen in some parts of the garden. Father Sun and Mother Earth could feel the sadness.

«How can I help my garden find its smile back?»
worries Mother Earth.

«I asked our friend the Moon for some advice,»
says Father Sun. «I will take care of it.»

Father Sun scans the garden when suddenly, he hears a little squirrel crying. «Hello Fluffy, why are you crying?» asks Father Sun.

«I am sad, and I feel all alone,» says the squirrel, «everything seems grey!»

«Oh! It's true that sadness often looks like big dark clouds,» replies Father Sun, «but did you know that there is a beautiful rainbow in your heart?»

Fluffy is puzzled. «How can there be a rainbow in my heart?» he asks.

«Come with me,» says Father Sun. «Let's find a calmer place, and I will tell you how to find it.»

Fluffy sat near a waterfall to listen to Father Sun talk about the rainbow.

Comfortably seated, he could hear the water flowing softly, and he closed his eyes.

«First of all,» says Father Sun, «inhale slowly while gently feeling your belly go out. Then, exhale slowly.»

«Again, Inhale, hmffffffffffff.
Exhale, pffffffffffff.»

Fluffy takes several slow and deep breaths.

Fluffy feels much more calm.
An orange elf appears before him and kindly addresses him.

«Imagine yourself at the top of a staircase,» says Orange.
«Go down the stairs slowly.»
7... 6.... 5..... 4...... 3....... 2.......1
«There, in front of you, is a door and we will open it together to discover a wonderful place.»

The squirrel feels good, and carefully listens to the elf. «Now,» says Orange, «imagine you arrive in a wonderful garden.»

There are beautiful trees, colorful flowers, and a peaceful river.
«Look at all those wonders before you!»

Fluffy goes on to discover other parts of the garden with the elf. He is taking his time to enjoy it as much as he can.

Then, Orange shows him the beautiful rainbow Father Sun told him about.

A beautiful orange light surrounds the squirrel.
He feels a lot of softness; just like the love of Mother Earth.

Orange then says to Fluffy;
«Anytime you feel like it; you can go
down these stairs again to come to this
wonderful place.»

«The light of your rainbow of wisdom
will help you push away the dark clouds.
Even if you cannot see it, this light is
always there in your heart.»

Father Sun gently caresses Fluffy
who slowly opens his eyes.
The clouds are gone!

Father Sun bids farewell to Fluffy and continues to stroll in the garden. His visit makes the shadier parts sunny again. They learn how going inside your heart can help you find your well-being.

That night, before going to bed, Fluffy thinks about the elf. He also thinks about the love of Mother Earth and Father Sun. Treasured by the Moon, the garden echoes with laughter and cries of joy.

Remember...

How can I find my joy?

When you take the time to meditate and go inside your heart to find your rainbow of wisdom, it helps you push away the clouds of sadness. Joy then reappears, like the sun after the rain.

What can I do if my sadness does not go away?

If sadness stays inside you for too long or comes back too often, share your feelings with an adult you can trust and who will listen to you.

Can meditation work for me even if I do not feel sad?

Whenever you feel the need to rest or calm down, take a moment to close your eyes and meditate, wherever you are. You can also meditate for the simple joy of feeling good!

Tools of the Heart

Fostering confidence and self-esteem

Colin Discovers Confidence

Grounding/Strengthening your self-confidence

Growing up often comes with its share of fears and hesitations.
Growing solid roots helps to build and nurture a positive self-confidence.

A storm is raging!
The wind shakes the oaks of the garden furiously.
Suddenly, an acorn is pulled loose and carried far, far away
from its home.

On its course, the acorn hits a rock and cracks open.
The seed inside falls onto the ground. Luckily, Mother Earth
welcomes it and covers it with all her love.

The little seed is happy. Mother Earth nourishes it, while Father Sun keeps it warm and cozy.

«My name will be Colin!» decides the little seed.

Father Sun and Mother Earth guide Colin in his growth and surround him with their presence and their love.

«The more I grow, the further I feel from Mother Earth!» notices Colin.
«Growing up can sometimes be scary!» he worries.

Colin is worried and cannot sleep.
He wonders what will happen when he becomes a bigger oak.

«What will happen to me?»
he asks the Moon, bright in the sky.

The Moon heard Colin and tells him:
«Inside your heart, there is wisdom,
which can help and guide you.»

«Wisdom!?» worries Colin,
«I have never seen any wisdom.»

«I will tell you how to find it,»
kindly answers the Moon.

Colin closes his eyes and carefully listens to the Moon.
«Focus on the love inside your heart,» she says, «and slowly breathe in.»

Colin relaxes.
He feels the calm settling inside him, and Yellow the elf appears before him.

«You see Colin,» explains the elf, «there is a lot of love and strength inside your heart, and it flows everywhere inside of you, just like your sap.»

Colin feels a sense of well-being and is filled with a beautiful yellow light growing inside of him.

«Now,» says the elf, «focus on the tips of your roots. They are firmly planted in the ground and in touch with the love of Mother Earth.»

Colin can feel his roots and all the strength flowing inside of him.

«You can feel this strength every time you need it,» says Yellow. «It will give you the confidence you need to grow up.»

Colin has grown and is now a strong young oak. He visits his heart often to meet with Yellow and to find his sense of well-being and self-confidence.

One morning, terrified birds are flying above Colin.
«A terrible storm is coming from the north of the garden!»
they chirp as they flee the storm.

Colin shivers, he sees the storm approaching, and he can
feel the fear rising within him.

Then he closes his eyes, focuses on his heart to gather all of his strength and confidence.

«My roots are solid,» he thinks, «and I won't fly away!»

When the storm arrives, Colin fearlessly stands it. The strong winds make him sway, but his roots are firmly planted.

He is really proud of himself.

Time has passed. In the garden, there is an oak swaying in the wind. He is not afraid of the furious winds or the storm. It is Colin stretching his branches towards Father Sun and his roots towards Mother Earth.

Remember...

Is it normal to worry sometimes?

Of course! It even happens to grown-ups you know! But the more your confidence grows inside you, the less space there is for fears and worries.

How can I make my confidence grow?

Inside of you, there is a lot of strength and courage but sometimes, you either forget about it, or you think it is gone. By remembering it is there, you can make your confidence grow again. It helps you become strong and confident, just like an oak who relies on its roots during a big storm.

Can I grow roots like a tree?

Absolutely! Close your eyes, breathe in slowly and imagine roots growing from your belly to the center of the Earth. Imagine the force rising inside you, from the bottom of your feet to the top of your head. You can grow roots anytime you need them!

Tools of the Heart

Fostering confidence and self-esteem

Colin and Fluffy Become Friends

Knowing yourself/Loving and appreciating

Positive self-confidence and self-esteem are the building blocks of healthy relationships; therefore, learning to appreciate who we are is a treasure for life.

It's a beautiful and sunny day.
Colin, the oak, is swaying in the breeze when he notices
a little squirrel happily coming his way.

«Hello!» says the squirrel.
«My name is Fluffy! What is your name?»
The oak blushes a little and timidly replies,
«I'm Colin.»

Suddenly, an acorn falls to the ground
and Fluffy looks at it with desire.

«May I eat it?» he asks.
Colin hesitates but finally accepts.

Colin observes Fluffy enjoying himself.
«That squirrel seems really nice,» he thinks.

«That was delicious,» says Fluffy,
«thank you very much! Goodbye!»

The next day, Fluffy comes back to see Colin.
«Hello Colin, I'm happy to see you!»

«Hello Fluffy! I'm very happy to see you too.
Would you like to eat an acorn?»

«Oh! I would love to,» answers the squirrel.
«It's very nice of you.»

Fluffy enjoys his gift while telling one of his
many adventures in the garden.

As the days pass by, Colin and Fluffy get to know each other. The oak trusts him more and more and really enjoys Fluffy's friendship.

The playful squirrel enjoys climbing in the oak and jumping from branch to branch. How nice it is to have a friend!

One morning, Colin is worried. Fluffy did not come to visit him as he usually does.

Time passes by, and sadness fills Colin's heart. He wonders if Fluffy forgot about him.

«Maybe it's because I have no more acorns to offer him,» he thinks. He tells Mother Earth about his sadness.

«Dear Colin,» says Mother Earth with love, «even if you don't grow any acorns right now, you are still a wonderful and kind oak.»

«But Fluffy did not come to visit me,» he cries. «Maybe he doesn't like me anymore!»

«And you,» answers Mother Earth, «what do you think about yourself?» Colin is confused, he doesn't know what to say.

Father Sun overheard everything.
He proposes his help to Colin.
«To answer your question, you first need to
breathe in calmly. Inhale... Exhale...»

Colin closes his eyes and breathes in
deeply. He can feel the calm settling in him.

Guided by Father Sun, Colin goes into his heart and thinks about his beautiful rainbow of wisdom.

Green, the elf, appears and kindly approaches him.

«Your heart is like a treasure chest,» Green explains.
«It holds your joy, your kindness, and your self-confidence.
When the chest is open, love can shine brightly, and you
can feel it.»

«But sometimes, when you think you're not loved anymore
or when you are sad and disappointed, it is like you are
closing the lid and you may feel less love.»

Colin carefully listens to what the elf is saying.
«You see Colin; you are the only one who can
open or close your personal treasure chest.»

«This inner treasure is wonderful, and no one
can ever take it away from you!»

«This treasure is YOU!»

Guided by Green, Colin imagines his heart
opening wider and brighter than ever before.

A calming and peaceful green light hugs Colin.
There is a lot of love and warmth.

«Even when Fluffy is not around, your treasure is
always inside of you. So are the happy moments
that you have spent with him.»

Colin is happy!
He now understands that he can
feel good about himself, even when
he is alone.

«Knock! Knock!»
Colin opens his eyes and is pleasantly surprised to see Fluffy.
«Here I am,» says the squirrel. «I took a long stroll in the
garden today. I have tons of stories to tell you!»

«Me too!» says Colin. «But there is a cold wind now.
Would you like to come up and take shelter in my leaves?»

Fluffy comfortably nestles in the oak.
The two friends are having a great time
chatting and laughing together.

The Moon thinks of how friendship is
such a wonderful thing!

Remember...

How do we become friends with others?

To do that, you must dare to open your heart to others so they can get to know you better. For that, you will need to grow bigger than your fears, trust yourself, but also, trust others, even if you are shy or scared.

Is it normal to be scared at first?

When you meet someone for the first time, you don't know what they might think of you. It can sometimes seem scary. But the more you get to know each other, the more your friendship grows, and the fear slowly fades away.

What is a true friend?

A true friend is someone who appreciates you the way you are. They enjoy spending time with you and wish you good. If a conflict happens, it's important to explain to your friend how you feel and to listen to how they feel, so you can find a solution that will please you both.

The Book Collection

Tools of the Heart
Fostering Confidence and Self-esteem

1. Father Sun and Mother Earth Create Life
Breathing/Finding your rhythm

Breathing is essential to life; conscious breathing is a simple, yet effective way to regain your calm and well-being by finding your body's rhythm.

2. Fluffy and the Rainbow in his Heart
Meditation/Finding your inner calm

Each one of us has a peaceful place inside their heart. Meditation is a tool that allows you to find your personal space or to go back to it.

3. Colin Discovers Confidence
Grounding/Strengthening your self-confidence

Growing up often comes with its share of fears and hesitations. Growing solid roots helps to build and nurture a positive self-confidence.

4. Colin and Fluffy Become Friends
Knowing yourself/Loving and appreciating

Positive self-confidence and self-esteem are the building blocks of healthy relationships; therefore, learning to appreciate who we are is a treasure for life.

5. The Choice
Insight/Listening to your intuition

Learning to listen to your inner voice and how to trust it, is learning to stay true to yourself in all situations.

6. Colin's Courage
Expressing/Confidence in yourself

Standing up for yourself is not wrong. It is about relying on your self-worth with confidence, to respectfully say what you need to say.

7. Enough is Enough
Self-respect/Daring to be yourself

Developing good communication skills also implies expressing your feelings and needs in a respectful manner, which can sometimes be a challenge!

8. Fluffy Finds his Well-being
Self-awareness/Taking responsibility

Growing up is also about becoming more aware of your emotions and learning to manage them responsibly.

The Meditation Collection

Tools of the **Heart**

Fostering Confidence and Self-esteem

Specially designed for young children, the guided meditations explore and develop the same themes, as seen in the **Tools of the Heart** book collection. These intend to reinforce the children's knowledge of themselves through their inner space of wisdom, where things can be seen, heard, and felt.

Meditation is also a wonderful tool that children can easily learn to help them self-regulate physically, mentally, and emotionally.

To learn more, go to our website:

www.toolsoftheheart.com